A Child of God

Stories of Jesus and Stewardship Activities for Children

by
Michael J. Caduto

Illustrated by
Adelaide Murphy Tyrol

Paulist Press
New York/Mahwah, N.J.

For the Children—
whose sense of wonder opens our eyes to the beauty of Creation

The song "All One Earth" is used here with permission of its coauthors, © 1994 by Michael J. Caduto and Steve Schuch. It appears on the musical recording *All One Earth: Songs for the Generations* by Michael J. Caduto (Norwich, VT: LunaBlu®, 1994), and in its companion book, the *All One Earth Songbook* by Michael J. Caduto (Norwich, VT: LunaBlu®, 1994).

The scripture quotations herein are the author's adaptation using a combination of *The New English Bible with Apocrypha* (Oxford Study Edition), Oxford University Press, 1976; *The Jerusalem Bible,* Doubleday, New York, 1966; and *The Holy Bible: The King James Version and The Revised King James Version,* Michigan Publishing Company, Grand Rapids, 1891.

Jacket design by Sharyn Banks
Text design by Lynn Else

Jacket and interior art copyright © 2005 by Adelaide Murphy Tyrol, with the exception of spot art on pages 25, 26, 34 and 35.

Text copyright © 2005 by Michael J. Caduto

Library of Congress Cataloging-in-Publication Data

Caduto, Michael J.
    A child of God : stories of Jesus and stewardship activities for children / by Michael J. Caduto ; illustrated by Adelaide Murphy Tyrol.
        p. cm.
    ISBN 0-8091-6726-3 (hardcover : alk. paper)
    1. Jesus Christ—Nativity—Juvenile literature. 2. Nature—Religious aspects—Christianity—Juvenile literature. 4. Christian education of children. 5. Christian education—Activity programs. I. Tyrol, Adelaide. II. Title.
    BT315.3.C33 2005
    268'.432—dc22

                                                                                    2005006097

Published by Paulist Press
997 Macarthur Boulevard
Mahwah, New Jersey 07430

www.paulistpress.com

Printed and bound in Mexico

Contents

Acknowledgments   iv

Introduction   v

Star of Salvation   1
Reflections   2
Activities   5
Starway to Your Story   5
Manger Menagerie   7
Celestial Celebrations   12

Miracles and Marvels   15
Reflections   20
Activities   21
Communi-Caring   21
I Am the Water   21
Aquatic Prayers   24
Aquatic Protectors   25

Birds, Blooms, and Blessings   29
Reflections   30
Activities   32
Animals of the Bible   34
Angels on the Wing   36
Giving Thanks   38

Glossary   41

Acknowledgments

This book has blossomed as a result of the faith and dedication of the excellent staff at Paulist Press, whose skills and attention to detail combined to produce a beautiful volume: Paul McMahon, Managing Editor, Susan Heyboer O'Keefe, Children's Books Editor, and Lynn Else, Layout and Design Department Manager. The stories seem to leap from the pages through Adelaide Murphy Tyrol's vivid illustrations. Steve Schuch's keen musical ear helped to flesh out the composition for the round called "All One Earth."

Reverend Roger Wharton (www.ecospirit.org), San Jose, California, and Deb Yandala, Chief Executive Officer, Cuyahoga Valley National Park Association, Peninsula, Ohio and Sunday School teacher, Prince of Peace Lutheran Church, Westlake, Ohio, both drew from a wealth of experience teaching youth about faith and the natural world as they generously reviewed the entire manuscript. My wife, Marie Levesque Caduto, who is an environmental educator and natural resource conservation specialist, read and commented on the many drafts that I dropped in her lap over the past year. Paul Feeney, a true child of God, encouraged me to keep this book at the forefront of my many writing projects. And I also thank the monks of Weston Priory—devoted disciples of Jesus Christ, whose gift of inclusiveness honors the Spirit of God in the natural world.

I am extremely grateful to those who gave of their time to facilitate, field test, and evaluate the stories, reflections, and activities with children: Dr. Stanley Cianfarano, Department of Education, College of St. Joseph, Rutland, Vermont; Alanna E. Greene and Pauline Hackett, Christ the King School, Rutland, Vermont; Sue LeBeau, who conducted the activities with various elementary schools in Monmouth County, New Jersey; and the staff of Assumption School, Millbury, Massachusetts: Sister Gertrude Lanouette, DHS, Principal, Jane Donovan, fifth grade, Jo Anne Holahan, sixth grade, and Kathleen O'Connor, fourth grade. Thank you all for helping this book come to life.

Introduction

God is the source in all of Creation. Every part of nature is a child of God. The compassion we feel for people can blossom into a care for the natural world. And nature has many faces. It is easy to befriend a bird or a butterfly, but it is by God's grace alone that we can even learn to love a mosquito.

Earth is a fragile home. We cradle the lives of every plant and animal in our hands. Without the clean air and water, the food and shelter that nature provides, no one could survive. Jesus reminds us, "Anything you did to the least of my brothers and sisters, you did to me" (Matt 25:40). Isn't a deer a brother; a flower a sister? The wildest things among us are the "least," the most helpless of all, the smallest of things.

Each chapter in *A Child of God* begins with a story that explores the life of Jesus and his close relationship to Creation. Although I have adapted and retold these stories, they preserve the details and truths found in the Bible.

Stories are followed by reflections about the nature of Jesus' life and the wisdom that can guide our relationship to God's Earth. The reflections also connect stories to the related activities. Every activity includes a set of instructions and a list of simple materials.

This book can be read and used directly by children in middle-to-upper elementary school (ages 8 to 12) and beyond. It can be shared across the generations. Teachers, parents, clergy, siblings, and friends can read the stories to younger children, answer questions, and adapt activities to their levels of understanding.

Read *A Child of God* and you will find new meaning in the life of Jesus Christ. Here is a unique and valuable resource for helping children of all ages to discover a life of faith, compassion, and caring toward every part of Creation.

Star of Salvation

(Matthew 2:1–12)

It was a still night in the quiet town of Bethlehem. A baby stirred where he slept in a small house. The twinkling light of the stars shined down on a mother and father who held hands as they lay next to the child.

Far away in Jerusalem, King Herod paced in his palace. He was disturbed by the spreading news that there was a new leader in his kingdom of Judea.

Herod was startled by the sound of a massive door knocker. Servants greeted three visitors and summoned them into the great hall to meet King Herod. The strangers were dressed in the colorful, elegant clothing from the East, marking them as scholars and students of the stars.

"Where is the child king that we have heard of?" they asked King Herod. "We are on a long journey and have followed his rising star."

"And why have you come here?" asked King Herod.

"We have come to worship him," they replied.

"I have heard rumors of this, this *child*," said Herod, his voice sharp with anger. "How can others claim that he is king of the Jews? I am the only king in this land!" he ranted.

In his rage Herod called together all of the religious leaders, historians, and those who followed the news in that region.

"Where can I find this 'Child King'?" asked Herod mockingly.

The group answered, "As the prophets have foretold, 'There will be born in Bethlehem one who will lead the people of Israel.'"

Herod collected his wits before he went back to meet with the visitors. "Come," said Herod as he motioned to the wise men from the East, the three Magi, in a voice now overly calm and reverent. "Come with me into my chambers."

When they had gathered around him, Herod quietly asked them when the star had first appeared. Then he said in measured tones, "Go to Bethlehem and search for the child. When you have found him, come back and tell me where he lies so that I, too, may worship him."

Again the three Magi set out on the road. They followed the star into the night as it led toward Bethlehem.

At last the star stopped in the sky above the place where the child was sleeping. The Magi were filled with hope to see the little house that was marked by the star. They arrived at the doorstep and knocked. Joseph opened the door, welcomed them in, and gestured toward Mary and the baby Jesus.

As soon as they saw the child with his mother, the Magi knelt down, bowed their heads and shed tears of joy. One at a time, they approached the child and offered gifts, which were wrapped in delicate embroidered tapestries. First came a gift of gold, the ancient sign of royalty. Next came the divine offering of frankincense. The third visitor opened his gift of myrrh to symbolize the passion of Christ that was yet to come. Mary, Joseph, and the three visitors from the East silently watched the child and wondered at the promise of his life as the rich scents of frankincense and myrrh filled the room.

In time, the Magi made their way back toward Jerusalem and King Herod. But it was a long journey and they stopped to rest for the night. As they slept an angel appeared to them in a dream.

"Do not return to King Herod," warned the angel, "for he plans to kill the child, Jesus." When the Magi awoke they were grateful to see that it was still nighttime. Under the cover of darkness they took a different road back to their homeland, one that led away from the city of Jerusalem.

Reflections

God could have sent Jesus to us as an adult who was ready to begin his work. Instead, God chose to introduce Jesus as a baby whom we would come to love. In this story the Magi have a childlike sense of wonder and excitement. They feel something in their hearts and put their worldly lives aside for a time to search for Jesus. Theirs is a journey full of mystery.

Who among us has the courage and wisdom to follow a star? How often do we trust in our faith so completely that we leave the comforts of home and set off on a journey to find some unknown that God is leading us to? God has a purpose and meaning for everyone's life. It is up to us to discover our true path, to follow the star before us, and to have the strength of spirit to complete the journey no matter who or what we meet along the way.

As we grow up our lives become cluttered with worries about getting high grades, being good at sports, pleasing parents, being accepted by friends, and, later in life, finding a job and making money. These concerns often cloud our feelings and prevent us from listening to our hearts, from enjoying our friends and family. Jesus understands and he encourages us to learn from children, whom he truly loves and blesses. He tells us that we must become like children to enter the kingdom of heaven, and reminds us that the kingdom of heaven belongs to little children (Matt 18:1–7 and 19:13–15; Mark 10:13–16).

Let us find and follow the star that will lead to Jesus and not allow our wants and worries to block the road that leads to a life of faith. When someone tries to steer us away from our own true path, let us pray for the wisdom and courage to do as the Magi did—*to go home a different way*. We can follow a path away from the trappings and temptations of the world, a path of love, faith in Christ, and service to all of Creation.

Activities

Starway to Your Story

MATERIALS: Map of circumpolar constellations, construction paper, colored pencils, crayons, pastels, markers, pencils, lined paper, materials as needed for the action you choose to honor your faith in Jesus. If you decide to paint your star story you will need water colors, newspaper to work on, brushes, containers of water, and rags for cleaning up.

Tracing the Starway

What is your story? Which star will you follow to Jesus? The sky is full of *constellations*— groups of stars that people connect with one another to form images.

Find a map of the constellations that you can see year round so that the star you choose to help tell your story will always be visible. These are called *circumpolar constellations*. Look for them in a guide to the stars at your local library, or go online to hometown@aol.com. Search under "circumpolar constellations" and click on your hemisphere: northern or southern.

In the northern hemisphere the circumpolar constellations include the Big Dipper in Ursa Major (the Great Bear) and Cassiopeia the queen, which is shaped like a W. Other northern circumpolars are Ursa Minor (the Little Dipper), Draco the dragon, Cepheus the king, Camelopardalis, and Lynx. There are many circumpolar constellations in the southern hemisphere, including Apus, Carina, Chamaeleon, Circinus, Dorado, Hydrus, Mensa, Musca, Octans, Pavo, Pictor, Reticulum, Triangulum Australis, Tucana, and Volans.

To find Polaris, which is also called the Pole Star or North Star, look at the Big Dipper. Imagine grabbing the handle and pouring water out of the far end of the dipper. The two stars that mark the path of the water as it pours are Merak and Dubhe—the Pointer Stars. Draw an imaginary line from Merak (in the dipper) through Dubhe (on the rim). Sight straight along this path for about five times the distance between Merak and Dubhe. Measure this by putting one finger on Merak and one on Dubhe. Keep those two fingers the same spacing apart and measure five times that distance in the sky to find the North Star at the end of the Little Dipper's handle.

Creating Your Story

Find the circumpolar constellations in the night sky or locate them on the map of the constellations. Now search for a star that draws you in. This will be your guiding star. Look at the stars that surround your star. Ignore the constellations that other people have created and imagine the night sky as a giant canvas waiting to be painted. What images do you see among the stars, such as animals, plants, or people? Draw the stars on a piece of construction paper and connect them to create the pictures that you see in the sky. Complete those illustrations and paint them or color them in.

Use these images to begin a story. Create an adventure! Tell the story of an experience that led you to have faith in Jesus. Share about how your faith has deepened as you've grown. Search for other images in the sky near your guiding star and use them to tell your story. Trust in the stars, in your imagination, and in the guiding hand of Jesus to help you create your story.

Continue your story into the future. Just as the Magi offered gifts to the Christ child, think of at least one thing you want to offer. This could be something that you say or do to directly honor Jesus. You can also choose to do something good for Earth and for other people. Once you have written the story of how you are going to live your faith, go out and do it!

Manger Menagerie

(A Puppet Play)

MATERIALS: Copy of script for the puppet show "Manger Menagerie," pictures of each animal to use as models for the puppets, construction paper, pencils, cardboard, crayons, felt-tipped markers, scissors, glue, tape, sticks on which to mount the puppets, table and old blanket or sheet for a puppet stage, props for the stage sets (palm trees, well and bucket on a rope, door at the inn, manger).

Jesus was born in the town of Bethlehem. He was laid in a manger because there was no room at the inn (Luke 2:1–7). Animals bore witness to Jesus' birth.

Imagine what the baby Jesus saw when he opened his eyes. There were his loving parents, Mary and Joseph, looking down at him. As his eyes wandered around the stable, Jesus saw the faces of cattle, sheep, and camels. When the animals came to the manger expecting to find food, instead they found a baby lying in the hay!

Animal faces were among the first that Jesus ever saw, so he probably felt like animals were part of his family, like brothers and sisters. We can imagine that Jesus had a fondness for animals the rest of his life.

Here is a short puppet show about Jesus' first moments in the manger, as seen from the eyes of the animals. You can also perform this as a play with extra people playing animals in the background.

In addition to a Narrator, seven characters appear in this story: Mary, Joseph, a donkey, the Innkeeper, Camel, Cow, and Sheep. If you present this as a puppet show, some puppeteers can do more than one character.

Prepare puppets on a stick of each character. Use blankets and a few props to create a puppet stage that includes all three scenes: a drinking well along the road with a bucket on the end of a rope, the door at the inn, and the stable of animals with a manger in the middle.

Practice the puppet show and use voices that you imagine each character would sound like. Gather an audience and perform "Manger Managerie."

Narrator: Over two thousand years ago, in the dark of night, a young couple named Mary and Joseph traveled to the town of Bethlehem. Mary was about to give birth to a child, so she rode on the back of a donkey which Joseph led by the reins. On the way, Mary and Joseph passed beneath palm trees. They stopped to drink from a deep well. Joseph pulled on a long rope and up came a bucket of cool water. He first gave the water to Mary, then drank some himself. At last they came to an inn and knocked on the door.

Joseph: Kind sir, can you spare a room for the night? My wife is heavy with child.

Innkeeper: No, I am sorry. All of our rooms are full. But you are welcome to sleep outside with the animals. That's the only space we have left.

Joseph: *(Looking disappointed)* As you wish. Thank you. *(Leads Mary over to the stables)*

Mary: At least we will be warm and safe for the night in the stable.

Narrator: Mary and Joseph walked over to an open courtyard next to the inn where the animals of the guests were kept for the night. As they lay down to sleep, Mary began to toss and turn.

Mary: Joseph, I think my time has come. The baby is almost here!

Narrator: Soon, Mary gave birth to a baby boy.

Joseph: We have a son! He's a handsome child. *(Brings some strips of cloth in which they wrap the child, then lays Jesus in a manger)*

Mary: *(Looks up at Joseph and smiles with a glow on her face, then kisses Jesus on the forehead)*

Jesus: *(Looks up at his parents, makes some baby talk, then looks around at the animals who are gathering: some cattle, sheep, and a camel)*

Camel: What is this baby doing in our food trough?

Cow: They must know we only eat grass and grains!

Camel: Of course. *(Looks into baby's eyes)* Whoah! There's something different about this little human.

Cow: What do you mean?

Camel: The way he looks at me; it's like he sees right inside and understands what I'm thinking.

Cow: What's in that hay you've been eating?

Camel: I'm not joking! Come over here and see for yourself.

Cow: *(Walks over, sticks his big head into the manger, and looks Jesus in the eyes)*

Joseph: *(Gently pushes cow away)* Shoosh!

Cow: *(Looks at Joseph)* Alright already, I'll MOOOOVE! *(Turns to Camel)* I see what you mean. His eyes are wise, like the eyes of an old man.

Sheep: I saw you two staring at that baby. Is it good news or BAAAAD?

Camel: Look for yourself.

Sheep: *(Stares into Jesus' eyes and keeps staring for a long time, in a daze)*

Jesus: *(Sneezes in Sheep's face)*

Sheep: *(Keeps on staring at Baby Jesus)*

Cow: Hey, Sheepy, don't get all woolly-eyed, it's just a baby.

Sheep: *(Shaking her head)* Wow, that's no ordinary baby boy. I discovered the meaning of my life while looking into his eyes.

Camel: Oh, right, the meaning of *your* life: Eat grass, chew, eat more grass, poop, make a lamb…

Sheep: *(Yelling)* Enough already! I'm *serious,* there's something unusual about that baby.

Cow: Yeah, like he's one of us, or like he's already met us or something.

Camel: *(Chewing his cud)* I know what you mean, like this kid is *wise.*

Sheep: I haven't heard him make any wisecracks.

Camel: No, I mean wise as in *wisdom,* man. Like, he's got it, you know? He understands.

Cow: Yeah, as if he were part of our family.

Sheep: Like he were part of every family.

Camel: *(Staring at baby Jesus)* I'd keep my eye on that kid. He's gonna go places. He's gonna be somebody.

Sheep: Then I wish he'd go someplace and be somebody soon so I could eat that hay he's using for a bed. You know how I get when I'm hungry.

Cow: Yeah, MOOOODY.

Celestial Celebrations

MATERIALS: "Star of Salvation" story, tables, plates, cups, napkins, utensils, materials needed for the projects chosen by those who will attend the celebration, copies of the music and lyrics to "All One Earth," musical instrument to play the song, teach the group, and begin on pitch.

Jesus told the disciples that whatever they asked for from God, Jesus would give to them in his name, and that the sight of him would bring great joy (Matt 18:19; Luke 11:9–10; John 16:22–24). Sometimes we forget that celebration is a holy time. God and Jesus are with us and rejoice to see us happy! Enjoying music, art, dance, food, and crafts are ways of letting them know that we are pleased with the many gifts we have received.

Reread the "Star of Salvation" story about the gifts of the Magi. Now gather together your friends, family, or classmates and plan a celebration—a mini-festival focused on the stars. Each person is to create or prepare something that is based on the theme of the stars and heavens. Don't forget, our sun is a star, too!

Ask everyone to describe what they would like to share at the celebration, such as a song, a meal, a dessert, an illustration, a dance, or a sculpture fashioned of wood or clay. Make sure there will be enough food and drink for the number of people who will attend.

Before the day of the celebration arrives, ask someone who is musically skilled to learn the song "All One Earth," which can be sung either as a two-part or four-part round. Make one copy of the song for each person who will attend the celebration.

On the chosen day, each person will come and share what they have prepared. Plan some time for each person to show the group what they brought and to say why they chose that particular thing. Songs, dances, and some other gifts will require time for presenters to lead the entire group.

Now share the gifts of food! As a concluding activity to your celebration, gather everyone together and sing the musical round "All One Earth."

All One Earth
a round

Words and Music by Michael Caduto
& Steve Schuch

1. We're on a cir - cle turn - ing free,

2. ev - er we're turn - ing toward the dawn in the East___ We are

3. all one Earth a fam - i - ly,

4. Let's help the Earth go 'round e - ter - nal - ly.

Miracles and Marvels

(Matthew 14:13–21; Mark 4:35–41, 6:30–44, 6:45–52;

Luke 9:10–17; and John 6:1–15)

When Jesus first began to teach he traveled far and wide in the land of Galilee, from hilltop to lakeshore, from the synagogue to the homes of the faithful and sinners alike. One day he cured the sick, the next day he shined a light on the lives of people whose spirits were caught in darkness. On hearing his words men and women mended their ways and cleansed their hearts. At Jesus' touch lepers were cured, blind people could see, and the crippled became healed. People marveled at the parables Jesus shared. His stories showed them the truth about their lives and revealed how to live in God's way, with caring and compassion. Jesus often stopped and talked with children.

One long day, after preaching to the crowds gathered along the shore of a lake, Jesus said to his disciples, "It is late and I am tired. Bring the boat and we will cross to a quiet place on the other side of the lake."

The disciples told the crowd to go home for Jesus needed to rest. They brought the boat along the shore to where Jesus was standing and he stepped inside. Jesus was so tired that he lay down, rested his head on a pillow, and fell asleep. A number of other small ships sailed with them.

A strong wind began to blow as the boats started to cross the lake and the air became charged with the scent of a storm. The wind grew stronger until a gale whipped at the waters. Heavy spray soaked the robes of the frightened travelers. Crests of tall dark waves crashed over the sides and began to fill the boats. Meanwhile, Jesus slept calmly in the stern.

Struck with terror by the raging wind and towering waves, and afraid they were going to sink and drown, the disciples panicked and woke Jesus.

"Master," they yelled over the roar of the wind, "if we take on any more water we are going to sink! Don't you care if we die in these angry waters?"

Jesus opened his eyes and stood up calmly. He peered down at the water filling the boat, then looked up into the howling wind.

"Peace," he said to the wind. "Quiet, Brother. Be still."

In an instant the wind stopped. Waves grew smaller and an eery stillness came over the lake. Rays of sun burst through the clouds and twinkled upon the quiet ripples. Water flowed from the boats as they rose to their full height above the waters.

In the silence that followed, Jesus saw the looks of amazement and awe upon the faces of his disciples. He opened his arms, gestured to the sky, and motioned out across the waters.

"Why do you shrink away like lambs? What would it take to cause you to truly believe?" Jesus again lay down, rested his head on the pillow, and slept.

Filled with dread and wonder, the disciples looked at one another. "What kind of man is this?" they whispered. "See how the wind and sea do as he commands."

Soon after this happened, Jesus and the disciples traveled to his home town of Nazareth, and then on to the surrounding villages where he continued to teach. One evening they sailed away to rest in a lonely place along the shore. But thousands of faithful who wanted to be with Jesus got there before they arrived. When Jesus and the disciples got out of the boat they found a large, hungry crowd waiting.

Sensing their yearning for his wisdom, Jesus taught the crowds for a long time, on into the late evening.

Then the disciples came to Jesus and said, "Let's send them home so they can eat supper. We have no food and we are far from any village."

"So get some food and feed them," said Jesus.

"You mean, go out and buy it with our own money?"

Jesus turned to the disciples and asked, "How much food do we have?"

"Five loaves of bread and two fish," his disciples replied.

Jesus looked up to heaven and blessed the food. He split the loaves, divided the fishes, and gave the food to his disciples so they could pass it out to the crowd. Every time the disciples ran out of food, Jesus provided them with more. The air filled with the smell of fresh fish and the rich scent of bread.

After everyone had eaten until they were full, the scraps of bread and fish were gathered up and filled twelve baskets. From meager rations, Jesus had fed a crowd of five thousand people.

"Now," Jesus told the disciples, "take the boat to a place known as Bethsaida on the other shore. I will remain here and send the crowd home."

The disciples rowed the boat against a strong head wind as they set out across the lake. Jesus, meanwhile, walked among the people. He touched children on the head and blessed them. He embraced the elders. Finally, Jesus turned to the crowd and bid farewell.

After Jesus sent the crowd home, he climbed a nearby mountain. Jesus kneeled there and prayed on into the cool, starlit night.

A little before the first light of dawn, Jesus rose and walked down the mountain. When he reached the lake he saw that the disciples had gone far from shore but that they were tired from battling against the wind.

Jesus gently stepped out onto the water and began to walk across the surface of the lake. As he came alongside the disciples, Jesus began to pass them by. But when they saw him walking on the water, they wailed in fear.

"Who could that be?" one asked.

"It must be a spirit," said another. "See how he walks on the water as if it were dry land."

Jesus turned and came toward the boat. "Do not be afraid!" he said to the disciples. "Don't you recognize me? It is I, Jesus."

Jesus stepped over the rails and into the boat. As the wind died down and the waters became still, the disciples fell to their knees, trembling.

"Arise and be glad," Jesus told them. "There is no need to be afraid."

But the disciples still were trying to understand how Jesus had fed five thousand people with a few loaves and fishes. And they found it even harder to grasp the new miracle they had just seen.

Reflections

How can Jesus calm the wind at his command? How can he feed five thousand people from five loaves of bread and two fish? Why is Jesus able to walk on water? Jesus has complete faith and a total sense of being connected to everyone and everything God has created. He knows that the wind and water are a part of him, and he of them. When Jesus enters Jerusalem and the people begin to sing and celebrate, and the Pharisees tell him to have his disciples stop the noise, Jesus says, "If these people fall silent, the rocks and stones themselves will cry out!" (Luke 19:35–40).

Jesus inspires faith simply by his presence. He once met a fisherman named Simon who had worked all night but caught nothing. Jesus tells Simon to go out and cast his net one more time. Simon does not think this will help, but he does as Jesus asks and pulls his net up bursting with fish (Luke 5:1–11). Even though there are times when we feel life is hard, the Bible reminds us that faith will bring abundance (John 21:1–13; Acts 14:16–18; Heb 11:1–3).

Jesus' faith is so strong, and his connection to Creation so complete, that anything is possible. When touched by Jesus, paralyzed people get up and walk and dead people breathe with new life (Matt 8–9; Mark 1–4; Luke 5–8). It is easy to look at the miracles Jesus performs and believe that those extraordinary things are only possible because he is the Son of God. Or, we can see ourselves as children of God and do good works of our own imagining.

We can use prayers and actions to make the world a better place. Jesus shows how to love God with all our heart, all our spirit, and all our mind. After that, the greatest commandment is to love our neighbors as we love ourselves (Matt 22:34–40; Mark 12:28–34; Luke 10:25–28; John 15:11–17). We are called to love those within our community and to respect others, even if their faith is different than our own (1 Pet 2:11–12). We can show our love by being kind and patient, honest and humble (1 Cor 13:4–7).

Activities

Communi-Caring

Jesus was an excellent communicator. We, too, can be loving and graceful in the way we act and speak toward others (1 Pet 1:13–16, 22–25, and 2:1–3). Good communication is like a dance: two or more people move in harmony with the words. Here are some things you can do to enter the dance:

- Choose your words carefully.
- Use words of respect, care, and support.
- Use humor to open hearts and minds to good things.
- Allow others to finish speaking without interruption so that you will better understand them and avoid arguments.
- Don't use words that criticize and belittle others.
- Whenever you have harmful thoughts, use *silence* to create time to think about what you are going to say. This will help you avoid sharing hurtful words and will allow space for helpful words and thoughts to come to mind.
- Communication is a circle that goes around between you and another person. Practice these three things with a friend, classmate, or family member: (1) Listen without interruption until the other person has finished sharing. (2) Reflect back to that person what you heard. (3) Ask that person to say if you are correct. Switch roles and repeat all three steps.

I Am the Water

Jesus spent a lot of time speaking to crowds along lakeshores. He drew strength from being close to the waters where many of his miracles took place.

MATERIALS: Either a natural area near the water to visit, or pictures and posters of beautiful aquatic environments and a large dark bowl of water. Also tape, tacks, copy of "I Am the Water" story, lined paper, pencils, clipboards. *Optional:* tape recorder, digital camera, computer, and PowerPoint® software.

Travel to a favorite place by the water near your home, learning center, or place of worship. If this is not possible, use pictures, posters, and artwork showing lakes, ponds, streams, rivers, or the ocean. Hang these up so you can see the many ways we use and experience water on our planet. Reflect on the story of "Miracles and Marvels" as you look at these scenic images.

Find a quiet cove, a tide pool, or some other place where the surface of the water is still. If you can't get to water in a natural setting, fill a large dark bowl with water and take it outdoors. Look at the surface of the water. See the reflection of the sky—the changes in colors, patterns, and textures. Look down at your own reflection.

It is no coincidence that we can see ourselves so clearly when we look into water. Jesus knows that we are connected to all of Creation, with God as our source. Water is all around us, and within us. About 80 percent of our body is water and nearly three quarters of Earth's surface is covered by water.

Find a comfortable place to sit for a time. Now read the following imaginary journey into the world of water. Better still, ask a teacher, parent, or group leader to read "I Am the Water" while you close your eyes and listen.

My journey begins in the sky. I am a drop of water that has formed around a tiny speck of dust in the clouds. More water condenses onto me until I grow so heavy that I start to fall. Down I go through the howling wind that blows in the cool whiteness.

With a hollow "ker-plunck" I land in a stream and begin to gurgle as I flow downhill. Small insects skitter across my surface and are snapped up by hungry fish. A leaf flutters down, lands on me, and rides downstream. It glides through quiet pools, turns in whirlpool eddies, bumps down rocky whitewaters, and crashes at the bottom of a waterfall that drops into a crystal mountain lake.

I drift in the slow-moving currents. At sunrise I warm up and rise to the surface. In the evening I cool and sink. It's busy on the surface. Fishermen glide past in boats, casting baited hooks into the water. Children swim and splash about. Birds fly in and land along the shore to take a drink and catch a meal.

One day a large fish swims through me and bites hard onto a hook. Thrashing its tail and leaping into the air, the fish pushes me all around as it fights for its life. I watch as it grows tired and bright colors fade from its silvery scales. Finally, a hand reaches down from the boat and lifts the fish out of me for the last time.

One early morning I drift close to shore where a ghostly haze swirls above me. Footsteps tromp down to the lake and shake me, causing ripples to roll out from shore. A young person kneels down and scoops me into a small cup. Now the child is drinking me and I flow down inside. It is warm and I can feel myself being absorbed. I flow here and there, becoming part of a human being. I am no longer the clear water I once was. I have become red blood that flows through streams of veins. I could be part of someone you've never met, or even somebody you know. Perhaps, some day, you will take a drink and I will become a part of you.

Reflect on Water

Here are some questions to ask about this experience: How did it feel to be a drop of water? Did you like being a single drop, or a part of something much larger, like the stream or lake? Why do you prefer one or the other? What was it like to watch the fish being caught? How did it feel when you became part of the person who drank your drop of water?

Write about Water

Is it safe to drink from a lake in the real world? Why not? Rewrite the story of "I am the Water." Make the drop of water flow into a river and through a city where it becomes polluted. Tell of how some children come down to the river, clean up the trash, and test the water to see if it is clean. Send the water through a treatment plant so it becomes drinkable.

Another version of the story could see the drop of water fall into the ocean. Act out the story and include sound effects that you create on a tape recorder. Or use a digital camera to take photographs of water scenes and use PowerPoint® to create a digital collage of your experience.

Aquatic Prayers

An old saying goes, "A great journey begins with a single step." For many journeys that first step is a sincere prayer. Some important steps we take as Christians, such as baptism, require clean, fresh water.

Prayer is often seen as a mystical experience because it is spiritual, but prayer also has a practical side. When we pray, we prepare ourselves and commit to take action. Prayers give us strength and guide us on our journeys. They help us to talk to God and walk the path we have chosen.

The act of praying cannot be separated from our actions. Practice these prayers while you do some activities from the aquatic projects that follow. Here are some simple daily prayers to help care for the waters:

morning: Remind yourself of the aquatic stewardship project you chose to do near your home (see "Aquatic Protectors"). Recommit to that project, for the sake of God, your own spirit, the spirit of the waters, and aquatic life.

noon: Take a moment for quiet prayer. Consider what you have accomplished that morning and what you need to do during the afternoon. Give thanks.

evening: Remind Jesus how much you love him. Thank God for the wonders of Creation and for giving you the ideas and strength for carrying out your project. Ask for help in seeing clearly what your next steps should be in order to do the best job you can with your project.

Aquatic Protectors

Freshwater is precious. Of all the water in the world less than 1 percent is the liquid freshwater that is found on the surface and underground. Most of this freshwater is found in the world's largest lakes, such as Lake Baikal in Russia, the Great Lakes in the midwestern United States, and Lake Tanganyika in eastern Africa. Only 5 thousandths of 1 percent of the world's liquid freshwater flows through our rivers and streams at any time.

Mapping

MATERIALS: Bible with historic maps of the Holy Land, atlas of your local area, large paper or posterboard for mapping, pencil, markers.

Open the Bible and read about other places where freshwater plays an important part in the stories, such as Exodus 7:14–25 and 17:1–7 and Numbers 20:1–11. Find the appendix containing historic maps of the Holy Land. Locate the lakes and rivers that appear in Bible stories you've read.

Take out an atlas and locate bodies of water in your region, such as rivers, ponds, lakes, or the ocean. Make a simple map showing these bodies of water and visit the ones found nearby. How clean are those waters?

Mentors and Monitors

MATERIALS: Trash bags, construction paper, poster board, ruler, pencil, scissors, permanent markers, tape, tacks, plastic file dividers for signs and posters, heavy gloves, paper bags or cardboard boxes for sorting recyclable and returnable cans and bottles, canoe or boat, life preservers, supplies needed for the conservation project(s) you choose, Internet access.

Contact some conservation groups in your area, such as a watershed association, nature center, and the branch of your government in charge of environmental quality. Make an appointment and bring the map you created in the "Mapping" activity. Ask about environmental projects going on in your surroundings and what needs to be done to clean up and protect the waters.

Form a group of friends, family, or classmates and get involved in local efforts to monitor and maintain the health of local waters. Log onto the Global Rivers Network at www.green.org and the Izaak Walton League of America's Stream Study Section at www.wsrv.clas.virginia.edu/~sos-iwla. Other Web sites to consult are: www.webdirectory.com (Water Resources and Pollution), www.epa.gov/surf and www.epa.gov/adopt. The International Rivers Network links human rights and environmental protection (www.irn.org).

Here are some specific projects you can do:

- Encourage people to conserve water. Place small signs in kitchens and bathrooms at home, in school, at camp, and at your place of worship.
- Put signs near storm sewer drains asking people to not throw garbage there.
- Eat only fish whose populations are healthy. (See www.webdirectory.com and click on "Wildlife" then "Fishes.")
- Volunteer for community recycling projects.

- Organize a "green-up" day to clean up litter at a local waterway. Ask your town to supply trash bags and give these to volunteers. Take trash and recyclables to your local landfill and recycling center. Redeem returnable bottles for money and donate this to a homeless shelter or food bank.
- Promote your clean-up project with flyers and posters that you design and display. Create a Web site and go on public access television and radio.
- Take a canoe or boat ride out on a lake or pond simply to enjoy being out on the water. *Arrange adult supervision and always wear a life preserver.*

Birds, Blooms, and Blessings

(Matthew 6:25–34, 7:7–8; Luke 12:22–32)

Jesus walked throughout the land teaching everyone who came to hear his words. His wisdom touched their hearts and spirits. In many places hordes of people gathered to listen.

One day when he saw that the crowd was growing into the thousands, Jesus climbed a tall mountain. With a motion of his hand Jesus hushed the murmur of their voices. Only the cry of a bird rang out and broke the stillness.

Then Jesus began to speak. He told his followers how they could live a new way, according to the word of God. Jesus taught about giving quietly to others and about how to pray to God in heaven. His wisdom rolled out over the crowds like waves breaking on the shore of a hungry sea. The multitude listened in awe and silence.

Jesus also told them to trust in God. "Do not fret about where you will find your next meal, or of what you are going to wear. Food is but one small part of life. Your heart and spirit are far more important than the clothes you wear on the outside. Will you live longer, or grow taller or stronger in spirit, if you spend time worrying about what you need for tomorrow?"

"Look up at the sky, and in the fields and forests. The birds do not have to plow, plant, and harvest or store their crops in barns. They find everything they need to eat in the food God grows for them. If God feeds the animals, do you think God will let *you* go hungry?"

"Do you see the birds flying with feathers as bright and colorful as the finest clothes? And what about the lilies that grow in the wild places? Even though they do not spin or sow, their petals are more fine and rich in color than the gilded robes of King Solomon. Their scents are sweeter than perfume."

"God gives great beauty and fragrance to flowers that live a short time, but are soon gathered and burned in the oven as fuel to bake bread. Don't you think God will take care of you?"

"Stop asking 'Where will my next meal come from? What will I drink? How are we going to afford new clothes?'

"God knows what you need! Tend to your spirit and look toward your time in heaven. If you seek justice in the world and grow the goodness in your heart, God will provide for your body.

"Do not worry about your problems or of what the future will bring. Live each day as the birds and flowers, singing the joys and painting the wonders of Creation. Have faith, and God will take care of tomorrow."

Reflections

God loves us so much that Jesus is sent to save the world (John 3:16–17). Jesus comes to save *all* of Creation, including the deer, the flowers, and all things wild. Jesus expresses his closeness to nature when he says, "Though foxes have dens and birds have nests, I, the Son of Man, have no place to rest my head" (Matt 8:18–20). Jesus compares himself to the animals because he, too, is at home in the wilderness.

Jesus knows that nature is a child of God. He shows us that we have a deep connection to all of Creation. Everything God makes is sacred because it comes from God and possesses the spirit of the Creator. The face of God exists in all of our neighbors, whether a tree, a bird, or a person.

Our faith in Jesus and our hope for the future are all built on love—the most powerful and lasting force on Earth (1 Cor 13:13). God intends for us to be saved and to play our part in saving all of Creation (Rom 8:18–25). He says that our purpose here on Earth is to love and serve our neighbors, especially those who are in greatest need. This includes our neighbors with wings and padded feet.

Birds are a special symbol of the Holy Spirit. When John the Baptist pours the water of blessing and baptizes Jesus, the spirit of God appears as a dove and comes from heaven to rest upon Jesus (Matt 3:13–17; John 1:29–34). The voices of birds are like angels; they call in the wilderness, celebrate God with their songs, and fill our spirits with joy.

Activities

Animals leap and fly from the pages of the Bible. Back when there were far fewer people in the world and the animals had plenty of forests, deserts, wetlands, grasslands, and other kinds of habitat in which to live, these species were abundant. They truly were the "multitude" that God created.

Animals that appear in the scriptures include:

Birds

bittern (little bittern and yellow bittern)

black kite (vulture)

black stork

crane

cuckoo

golden eagle

great-horned owl

griffon vulture (Eurasian griffon), often referred to as "the eagle"

hoopoe (European)

lanner falcon

ostrich

pelican

purple water-hen

raven

red kite

ring dove (ring-necked dove)

turtle dove

white stork

Mammals

bactrian camel (2-hump)

badger

Barbary ape

bear (Syrian bear)

dromedary camel (1-hump)

elephant

goat

hippopotamus

horse

hyrax

leopard

lion

rhinoceros

roebuck (red deer)

sheep (broad-tailed)

Syrian fox-jackal

wild ass

wolf (gray)

Reptiles, Insects, and Others

adder

crocodile

locust

palmer-worm or pilgrim-worm (caterpillar)

scorpion

viper

Animals of the Bible

MATERIALS: Books and articles about wildlife that include Bible animals, pencil, notebook of lined paper, construction paper, poster board, scissors, tape, stapler, crayons or markers, ball of yarn, television, DVD or VCR player, videos or DVDs of movies with Bible animals in them, Internet access, other supplies as needed to carry out your chosen conservation projects.

Learn about Bible Animals

Gather a small group of your friends, family, or classmates. Choose some Bible animals that you want to know more about. Collect books and articles at the library and visit the Internet. Discover what those animals look like, what they eat, how they behave, what kinds of sounds they make, and what kinds of habitats they need to survive. Some good Web site search engines are Internet Explorer, Netscape.com, and Google.com. Consult the list of endangered species and their descriptions on line at ECES (EarthCrash EarthSpirit). Also, call up WebBible.net, scroll down to "Encyclopedia" and click on "Animals."

Find and share some movies that have Bible animals in them.

Record your findings in notebooks about Bible animals. Write the name of one animal at the top of each page and its information below. When you are done, bind all of these pages into a report called "Animals of the Bible."

Use what you've learned to:

- Draw pictures of Bible animals.
- Practice mimicking the sounds those animals make.
- Play a game of charades by acting out an animal and having others guess which one it is.
- Create a food web. Have each person become an animal and sit in a circle. Use yarn to connect animals that eat each other, and are eaten by each other. See how complex the

web becomes! Once the web is done, have everyone pull gently on the yarn. Then have a few animals let go to symbolize their extinction. What happens to the web? What does this mean for how important each species is in the web of life?

Protect Endangered Animals

Find out how Bible animals are faring today. Consult www.webdirectory.com, click on "Wildlife" and then "General Endangered Species," or click on a specific group of animals.

What actions can you take to help endangered animals survive? Work with your group to create a poster board display for the religious education bulletin board or the display area at the camp nature center. Create pictures of the endangered animals you've learned about. Include descriptions of projects that your team, and others, can do to help those animals most in need.

Now get involved with some of the projects you thought of in your report, as well as those described by conservation organizations that are working to protect these animals, such as the World Wildlife Fund, the National Wildlife Federation, Defenders of Wildlife, and the National Audubon Society. Use your notebook to keep track of all you do for the animals.

Angels on the Wing

Angels are mysterious creatures that soar in our imaginations. Often they are pictured as human-like beings with broad, feathered wings. It is not surprising that angels are seen as bird-like. Aren't birds examples of God's powers of wonder, of our Creator's love for beauty, song, humor, and life?

The more we learn about the natural world, the better we can observe and appreciate birds as God's work. With practice we can begin to see and enjoy the endless variety of colors, shapes, sounds, and behaviors of the birds in our own neighborhoods. This is a good project for older children to work on together, and to then conduct for younger children.

MATERIALS: Binoculars, field guide to birds of your region, recordings of the calls of common songbirds, CD/cassette player, pencil, notebook, clipboard, or cardboard backing for writing.

Bird Watching

Do you know a friend, classmate, or family member who likes to go out and watch birds? If so, ask that person to take you along the next time he or she goes bird watching. Or you could go to any of your local nature centers, Audubon sanctuaries, and parks that offer bird-watching trips.

Bird watching is very simple. All you need is a pair of binoculars, a pencil, a notebook, and a field guide to birds that live in your area. Local libraries usually have a good selection of field guides. The more you go bird watching, the more you'll learn about the ways that you can identify them. Don't forget to simply enjoy their songs, their beauty, and grace on the wing!

Gather together a small bird-watching team, some binoculars, and field guides to bird watching or "birding." It is good to have at least one experienced "birder" along to help with identification. Take a slow, quiet walk through the habitat in and around your home, school, camp, or place of worship.

Once you see a bird, look it up in your field guide and identify it. Write in your notebook the different species of birds that live in or travel through your local environment. You may be surprised at how many different birds are living around you. Draw in your notebook the things that you notice the most, such as the shapes of beaks and feet. Describe the habitats where the birds live, what they are eating, and what their songs and calls sound like.

Here are some of the things to look for:
- size
- color
- shape (wings, tail, feet, beak or bill, overall outline of body)
- songs and calls
- habitat (forest, shrubs, grassland, desert, field, freshwater, seashore…)
- field markings and distinctive patterns, such as eye-rings, stripes, and wing bars; tail patterns; and rump patches
- flight patterns (straight and steady, rise and dip, soar, hover…)
- behaviors (tail wagging, swimming, wading, climbing tree bark…)

Now go to the library and take out a collection of bird songs recorded on cassette or CD. Listen to the songs of the birds you have seen. Play these calls often to help you remember them. Practice identifying these calls outdoors.

Take a number of bird-watching expeditions during different seasons. Record in your notebook the list of the birds you see as well as your field notes and drawings from each trip.

Giving Thanks

Gratitude is one of the greatest gifts we can return to God. Even nature gives thanks for God's creative spirit. John the Apostle heard Earth crying out to the Lord, "Every living thing in heaven and on earth and under the earth and in the sea cried, 'Praise, honor, glory and power to God and to Jesus, the Lamb of God, forever and ever'" (Rev 5:13–14).

MATERIALS: Supplies will depend on the specific projects you choose to get involved with for helping birds, Internet access.

Express your gratitude to God for giving us the amazing creatures we call birds. Start by doing something to help birds. A great resource for creating a bird habitat in your own yard is the *Audubon at Home: Gardening for Life* guide at www.audubon.org/bird/at_home/. Start very simply with a bird feeder and birdbath. Get involved at home with Project FeederWatch (http://birds.cornell.edu/PFW/), or get involved in school with Classroom FeederWatch (http://birds.cornell.edu/CFW/). Find out about endangered birds and how you can help to protect and save them.

Start a collection of books, stories, movies, art, music, or other creative forms of expression inspired by birds. Share your own artistic appreciation for birds: write a poem or story; create or sing a song; draw or paint a picture. Hold a festival to celebrate birds. Let your imagination take flight!

Glossary

celestial Something in the sky or in heaven, or that is spiritual or divine.

circumpolar constellations Constellations (groups of stars) found in the polar regions that we can see year round.

conservation To take care of nature and the resources we receive from the natural world through actions like recycling, saving energy, and preservation.

endangered species A species that has so few members left it is in danger of becoming extinct, of disappearing forever.

frankincense Frankincense smells pleasant when burned. It is made from the gummy sap of certain trees in the genus *Boswellia* of Asia and Africa.

habitat The home environment of a plant or animal, such as a forest, desert, ocean, river, field, or pond.

head wind A wind that blows opposite the direction something is moving.

Holy Spirit (Holy Ghost) The spirit of God; third person in the Holy Trinity.

locust Large grasshoppers that, as adults, often move in swarms of millions that strip plants of their leaves and destroy crops; of the genus *Schistocerca*.

Magi Three wise men from the East who made a pilgrimage to Bethlehem to worship the baby Jesus.

manger A small crib or trough filled with food for animals. An open courtyard next to an inn where travelers leave their animals for the night.

myrrh Myrrh—used as incense and in scented oils—is from the sap of trees and shrubs in the genus *Commiphora* of Arabia, India, and eastern Africa.

Pharisees Ancient Jewish peoples who lived by the strict laws of Moses.

salvation　　To be saved—to have your soul delivered from sin and evil. To live by the virtues of love, life, and truth.

scriptures　　Sacred books; the writings and readings from sacred books.

species　　A particular kind of plant or animal that can only reproduce with each other. For example, the golden eagle is one kind of species.

stewardship　　To protect and care for all of God's Creation—Earth and Sky. To do God's will in service to the natural world and humankind.

wilderness　　A place where nature is wild and free from the marks of people.